ROMAN TO THE RESCUE

Written by
SOPHIE STARR

Illustrated by
BEN BARTER

"Oh no! Where am I?" Sophie cried into the night.
She didn't know where she was, what a terrible fright!
"I'm lost in this storm, and I can't find my way out!"
The forest was dark, her mind filling with doubt.

Then all of a sudden, she saw two little ears

Sticking out from behind a bush; Sophie quickly wiped her tears.

She snuck over to the bush and slowly peaked over to see,

What was hiding there? And to her surprise...

A LITTLE PUPPY!

"AHHHHH!" Sophie screamed! "AWOOOOOO!" the puppy replied.
Sophie said, "You scared me so much, but you don't need to hide!
How did you end up in a bush in the woods all alone?
Are you lost in here too with no way to get home?"

The pup looked up at her with the cutest eyes she'd ever seen,
And she knew she had to help him, whatever that would mean.
"I'm gonna call you Roman!" and he gave a great yodel in reply,
"I'll take care of you, I promise." And right then her tears were dry.

Together Roman and Sophie found their way out of the woods,
And Sophie took Roman home like any best friend should.
They'd survived this adventure, what was next on the list?
All kinds of life lessons with Roman there to assist!

Roman taught Sophie about compassion and responsibility,
Selflessness, playing fair, being present, and humility.
Roman showed her how to trust others, and even herself.
And how love was not something to tuck away on a shelf.

When Sophie was sad or didn't know what to do,
There was her best friend Roman, to the rescue!
Sophie had found a best friend and someone to care for,
Even on days when caring for herself was quite a big chore.

She bathed him and loved him
and gave him her food,
Roman needed Sophie's help,
whether she was in a good or bad mood.

She had someone to care for and
this gave her purpose,
And showed her that love is much more
than what we feel on the surface.

Love isn't just a feeling or what we see with our eyes,

It's the way we treat others, of any shape, of any size.

Love lives in our actions,

in the things that we do,

Love is also the way

we take care of ourselves too.

When danger would call,

or when times got too hard,

Roman took his position,

in front of Sophie, standing guard.

They slept side by side,

not a night did they miss,

And Sophie's alarm clock was

a big sloppy KISS!

Time marched along,
and the two of them grew,
And wherever Sophie went,
there was her little boy too.

Through life's ups and downs,
Roman stayed right by Sophie's side,
And helped her to take every high
and every low in good stride.

SEEDS

"The lessons he taught planted seeds in her heart,

That grew into a beautiful field for him to play in when they part…"

I Don't Wanna Get Up

I don't wanna get up.
Not right now, not today.
I will stay here in bed,
And I'll stay here all day.

If I do not get up,
Then nothing can start.
Not my chores, not my worries,
Not my strange mixed-up heart.

I have homework to work,
And a whole room to clean.
I must worry my worries,
'Till they burst at the seam.

I must be a good girl,
And make everyone proud.
Be happy and joyful,
But not be too loud.

I must solve all my problems,
As quick as a wink.
I must have all the answers,
But not overthink.

There is too much to do
In this big to-do day,
So I'll stay here in bed,
And I'll stay here all day.

But what about Roman?
What on Earth will he do?
If I stay here in bed
'Till the whole day is through?

He won't go for his walk,
He won't even be fed,
He won't run, jump, or play
If I stay in this bed.

I don't wanna get up.
Not right now, not today.
But up I must get,
Come on Roman, LET'S PLAY!

Why Did You Bite Me?

OUCH Roman! You bit me!
With your little puppy teeth!
But you don't look mean and angry,
Is there something underneath?

What could this bite mean?
What could it speak for?
Did you hurt me on purpose?
Or was it something much more?

I've bitten people too,
Well, not really a "bite."
I've bitten people with words,
'Till they're filled up with fright.

When they're scared of my bite,
Then they leave me alone.
And I cannot be hurt,
By myself, on my own.

Is that why you bit me?
Are you afraid too?
Are you protecting yourself
From what people can do?

Maybe we all bite a little
When we're scared and confused,
And we can tell those who bite us,
"I've bitten people too."

Maybe next time I'm scared,
I can say it out loud-
Let out a deep breath,
And turn my fear into a cloud.

Then the cloud can float away,
And I'll feel a bit more alright,
And I won't hurt anyone
With my words that can bite.

I don't know why you bit me,
But this much is true:
I know what it's like,
To have bitten people too.

Difficult To Love

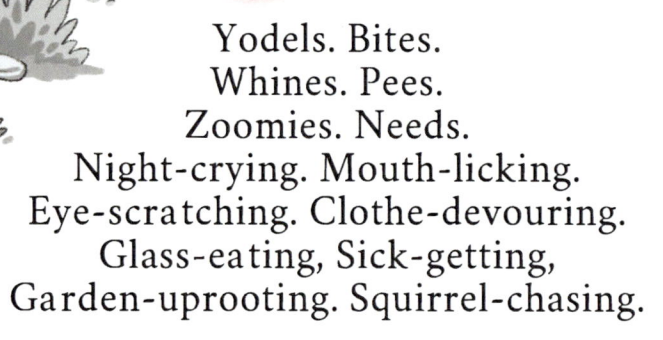

Yodels. Bites.
Whines. Pees.
Zoomies. Needs.
Night-crying. Mouth-licking.
Eye-scratching. Clothe-devouring.
Glass-eating, Sick-getting,
Garden-uprooting. Squirrel-chasing.

The things you do are difficult.
They make work for me to do.

But, sometimes these difficult things
Are my favorite things about you.

You are difficult,
But you are not difficult to love.

And if all that is true,
Maybe that means
I'm not quite so difficult to love too.

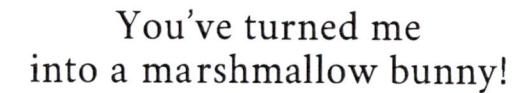

Marshmallow Bunny

You've turned me
into a marshmallow bunny!

A cotton ball chinchilla.

A big hot fudge snuggie.

I was grumpy.
I was sharp.
I was selfish.
I was proud.
I don't know why.

Everything else in this
life had hardened me,

Until

You turned me
into a marshmallow bunny.

Different

A lady and her baby were sitting on the bus,
And of all the places, right beside the two of us.
We had different clothes, different hair, different languages, different skin.
We had been told many times that they didn't like anyone foreign.
You were hidden in my bag, it was a secret you were there,
But after several hours, you wanted to come up for some air.
I felt a furry tickle and through the zipper popped your head!
We were only halfway there, and you got a little too excited.
"Oh no!" I thought, "What will the baby next to us do?"
Before I knew it, she was reaching out her hand to pet you!
I looked at her mom and saw a twinkle in her eye,
As she watched her baby tap you on the head to say "Hi."
You yodeled hello, and a smile on the baby's face appeared,
I looked at her mom again and she was smiling from ear to ear.
For the rest of the bus ride, you and the baby played
And the longer we shared this moment, the less I felt afraid.
We spoke different words, couldn't speak the same language.
We were two different rivers, but Roman you were the bridge.
Without you, we would have sat in silence on the bus for miles.
We wouldn't have shared the knowing looks, the laughs, or the smiles.
We might have been different, but we were both still human.
Sharing a funny bus ride while her baby played with you was the solution.
We got off the bus and went our separate ways,
This core memory with you is one of my favorite days.
It was a lesson learned: imagine how much time could be spent
Laughing together, instead of worrying about being too different.

You In The Shoe

Remember when I lost you for a whole entire day?
I thought you'd run off, right into danger's way!
I was worried and panicked and made a decision:
I will stop at nothing to find Roman - this is my mission.
You weren't with the goats, or sniffing around the well.
You weren't in the bushes, not as far as I could tell.
"ROMAN WHERE ARE YOU?!" I shouted and cried.
I just could not give up, so I went back inside.
I retraced my steps and looked at the closet door,
Even though my brain was telling me "you've looked here before."
I looked all the way up and looked all the way down,
And there at the bottom, was a furry bit of brown.
My heart burst as I got closer, praying it would be true,
AND IT WAS! I FOUND YOU! SLEEPING RIGHT IN MY SHOE!
I breathed a sigh of relief, my first real breath that day.
I was so scared when I lost you, I just had to get out of my own way.
In fact, this was the first time, to my great disbelief,
That I wasn't stuck in my head all day, and it was such a relief!
Maybe I should get unstuck more often, maybe it's true,
As long as you promise to only get lost in my shoe.

Away

Where does my love for you go when you go away?
I need somewhere to put it, somewhere it can stay.

It won't fit on the shelf, or under the bed.
It won't fit in my closet, or on top of my head.

I have nowhere to put it, so where should it go?
Maybe here in my heart, maybe here it can grow.

One rainy day,
Sophie woke up with a start.
Something didn't feel right
deep down in her heart.
It was a storm like the one she'd
found Roman in years ago,
When he'd rescued her in the woods,
her real-life hero.

Sophie looked for her Romy boy,

she looked high and low.

Down every street, every alley,

and in every window.

Sophie looked up and down

and all around in a hurry,

But the more she looked,

the more she started to worry.

After searching all day Sophie went back to the forest,

Where she first had found Roman and had made him that promise.

"Oh no, where are you?!" Sophie called into the night,

The forest animals looked on sadly at the poor girl's great plight.

Soon the birds sang a song that sounded more like a cry,

And Sophie knew in her heart that this was some sort of goodbye.

Roman was somewhere different now, but she didn't know what different meant,

Didn't know where different was, or how far different went.

She wasn't ready to say goodbye to her sweet Romy boy.

He had taken nothing with him; not his bone, not his toy.

They hadn't had enough cuddles, enough walks, enough time.

Goodbye felt like it stole him, it felt like a crime!

Sophie sat by a pond
and had herself a big cry.
Inside her a thunderstorm, hurricane,
and tornado began to fly.
"I'm lost in this storm,
and I can't find my way out."
Sophie cried into her hands,
her mind filling with doubt.

When she wiped her tears away, she saw her reflection in the pond,

And there was her Romy boy! Joining her from beyond!

Sophie's heart was a big field, and her best friend was there,

Playing, running, and jumping high up in the air!

"Roman! You found me
in the forest again!
You snuck into my heart!"
Roman nodded yes to his friend.
"But how can I take care of you now
if you're in my heart here?"
Roman didn't answer,
just tilted his head up to hear…

"Well if you live in my heart,
then what I must do

Is take care of my heart,
since you'll be in there too!"

Roman gave a great big
"AWOOOOOO!"
to say yes in response,

And Sophie knew what to do,
all of a sudden, all at once.

Sophie realized that Roman wasn't really that gone,

He is always with Sophie; in her heart he lives on.

The lessons he taught her planted seeds in her heart,

That grew into a beautiful field for him to play in when they part.

By taking care of her heart and keeping out the weeds of hatred,
She was taking care of Roman too, and the field where he waited.
By letting go of bitterness, self-pity, resentment, and fear,
Maybe Roman will want to stay in this field in Sophie's heart here.

Sophie smiled at her reflection as Roman looked up at her,
The storm moving away from the spot where they were.
Before leaving the forest, Sophie blew a little kiss,
And told herself and her Romy boy, "I'll take care of you, I promise."

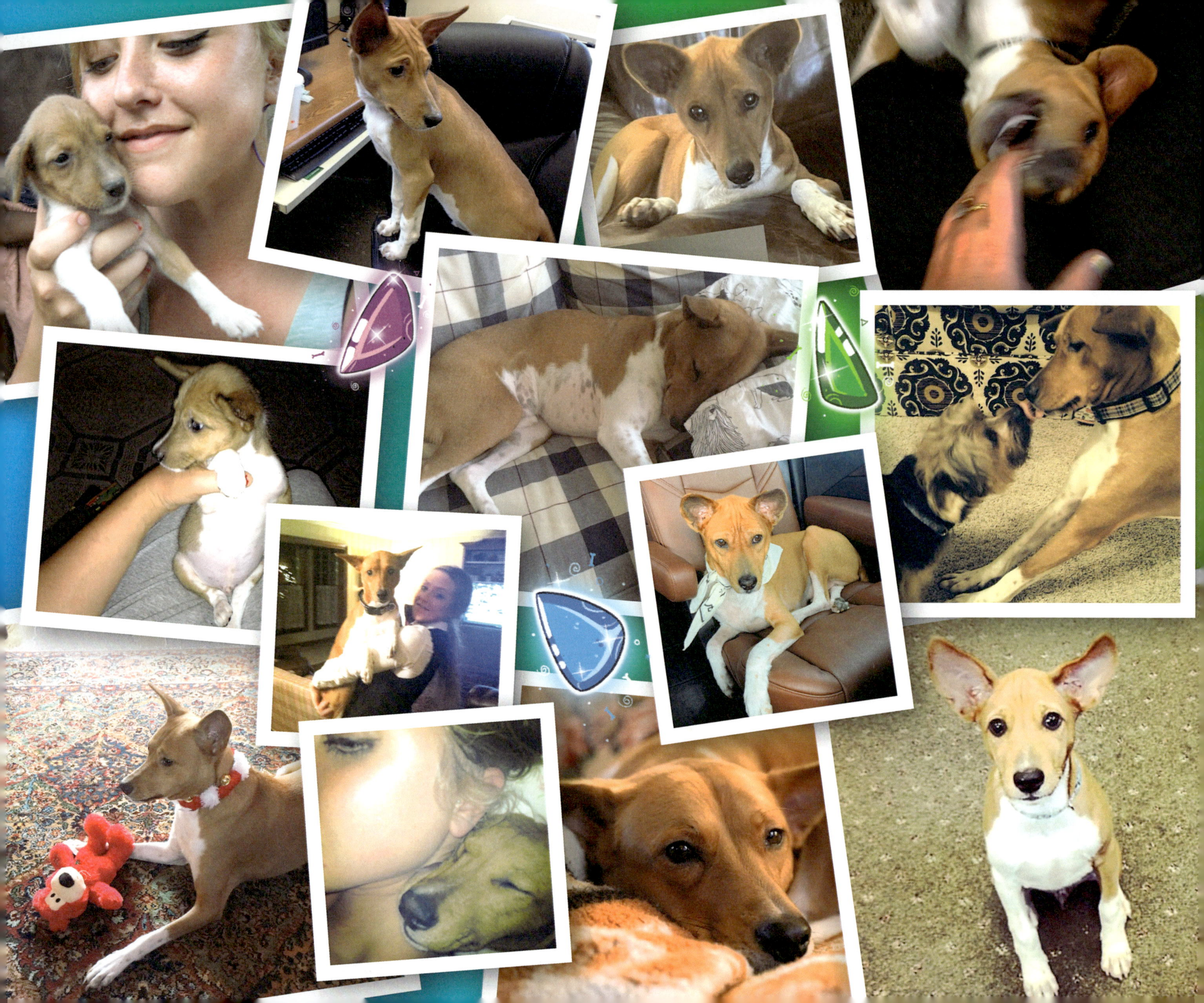

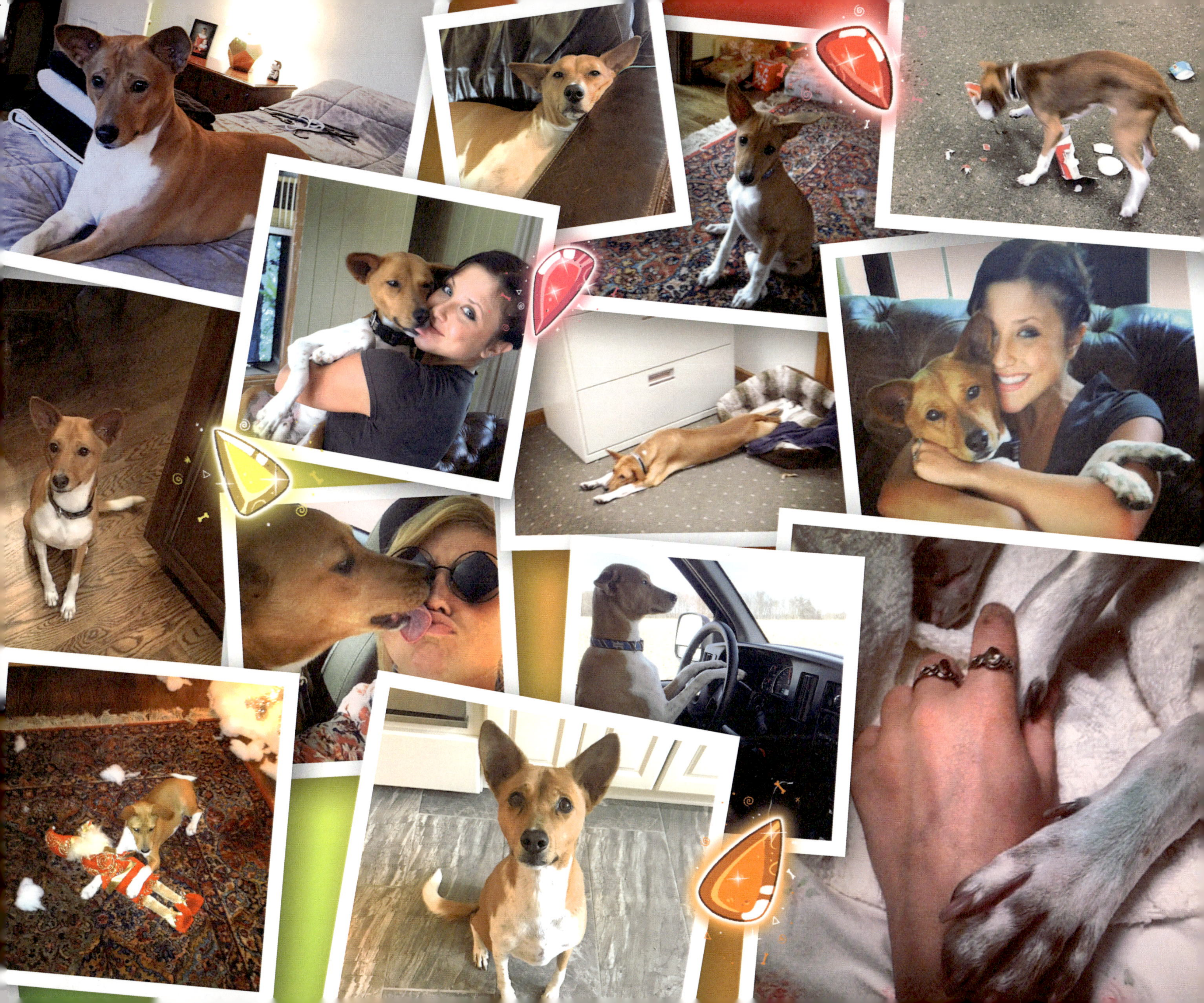

About the Author (Sophie) and Roman

You found us! I'm Sophie, the author of and character in this book, and Roman was really my dog! I wasn't a little girl when I met Roman, but I did find him during a stormy time in my life in Ghana, West Africa. Roman helped me overcome some of the most difficult times in my life, and the stories in this book are based on the true stories of our time together and the lessons Roman taught me. Roman continues to help and guide me to this day through these lessons and the love he gave me while he was here. From the very bottom of my heart, thank you for reading this book and for letting me share my Romy boy with you. Now that you know who Roman is, he feels a little less gone. We should all be so lucky to have a Roman in our lifetime.

If I may, I would like to encourage anyone who finds this book to adopt not shop when looking for your next pet, and to always spay and neuter. These two actions greatly reduce animal suffering, and to further that cause, a percentage of the proceeds from your purchase will go to animal rescues around the world.

> *"Someone told me once that dog is God spelled backwards. Maybe God created the animals so we could be closer to Him. Thanks be to God for Roman and for all of our furry friends."*
> – *Julie Starr*

Acknowledgements

Camille Jun,

For her encouragement and support as a friend throughout this process and for being an integral part of the creation of this book, which would not exist as it does without her direction and assistance. Roman would have given one of his best yodels to you.

My parents Nick and Julie,

I could not have found and brought Roman home without you. You gave me the greatest gift of my life. Thank you for loving him.

April,

If a Nobel Prize existed for animal caretakers, it would surely go to you.

A special acknowledgement to all the people and children in Ghana who left me better than when they found me, specifically the Gaisie family, Diana, Martha, Abraham, Enoch, and Moses. To everyone at Amanda Animal Hospital, Ohio State Veterinary Medical Center, and MedVet Columbus.

Illustrated by Ben Barter at Beehive Illustrations

Designed and created by Emily Hunter-Higgins at Beehive Illustration